I'M JUST LIKE YOU

By ROBERT J. MOORE

Illustrations by Chy Suzuki

I'm Just Like You
By Robert J. Moore

The story begins...

2

Once upon a time in a friendly town, there were children of all shapes, sizes, and colors. They went to the same school, but sometimes, things were not as happy as they seemed.

4

Meet Emma and Noah, two friends with different looks but hearts that beat the same. They loved playing games, sharing stories, and laughing together.

One sunny day, a new friend named Chloe joined their class. She had a different hairstyle, wore different clothes, and spoke a language they didn't know.

8

Emma and Noah were curious. They asked Chloe about her favorite games and the places she came from. They learned that Chloe loved many of the same things they did.

10

But, not all the children were as kind. Some of the kids started whispering unkind words and pointing fingers at Chloe because she looked different.

Emma and Noah didn't like seeing their friend sad. They decided to stand up against the unkind words and teach everyone that being different is what makes each of them special.

14

As days passed, the kids in the school began to understand that being different was something to celebrate. They realized that they were all unique, just like the colors of a rainbow.

16

The school decided to have a special day to celebrate everyone's uniqueness.

Children brought dishes from their cultures, wore traditional clothes, and shared stories about their families.

18

In the end, the children learned a valuable lesson — that the true beauty of friendship lies in accepting and celebrating the differences that make each of them special.

20

Dear Friend,

No Matter how you look or where you're from, remember that we are all special in our own way.

Let's stand up against unkind words and celebrate the beautiful colors that make us who we are.

The end of our story, but the beginning of a world where people come from different backgrounds but together are like different flowers that make a beautiful garden. Remember, no matter how different we may seem, we are all connected in this BIG World full of beautiful people. Just remember, I'm Just Like You.

ACKNOWLEDGMENTS

Writing *"I'm Just Like You"* has been a journey that reflects my love for both storytelling and the education of young minds. For over 20 years, I've had the privilege of teaching and working within the community, shaping the lives of countless children. These experiences have taught me the importance of empathy, understanding, and the power of connection—values I've poured into this book.

To my students, past and present, thank you for being my greatest teachers. Your curiosity, resilience, and joy inspired every word. To the parents, teachers, and community members who nurture young minds daily, this book is for you as much as it is for the children.

Finally, to my family and friends, your unwavering support throughout my two decades of writing has been a constant source of encouragement. Thank you for believing in my dream and helping me bring this story to life.

DEDICATIONS

To my beloved children,

Though we've faced difficult times, there are so many reasons to celebrate. As I move forward in life, I hold hope that we all grow closer, cherishing the moments we have left on this earth. Each of you has been an inspiration for this book, reminding me of the beauty and strength within our family.

To my prayer family—544 days today, August 30, 2024, and counting—you have changed my life. I asked for clarity, and God delivered. Thank you.

With love and gratitude.

I'm Just Like You

By Robert J. Moore

Illustrations: Chy Suzuki

Editor: Anelda Attaway

Published by Jazzy Kitty Publications

Wilmington, Delaware

877.782.5550 - http://www.jazzykittypublications.com

anelda@jazzykittypublications.com

Copyright © 2024 Robert J. Moore

ISBN 978-1-965381-05-2

PRESENTS

Robert J. Moore, affectionately known as, Coach Rob has a heart for the kids, and a passion for serving the community. He has become a Teacher, Advocate, and Role Model for countless children over eleven years. Coach Rob is the son of the beautiful and loving Florence Moore but, was adopted at age 11 by Christopher Michael Smith. His relationship with with his mother remained strong but, he soon moved to Philadelphia in 1990 and attended Saul High School. Then, graduated from Maryland Eastern Shore in 2000. He is the father of 10 children, BUT is dad to hundreds of kids throughout Wilmington, Philadelphia and Baltimore.

In 2006, he relocated to Delaware and founded the C.H.A.N.C.E Foundation (Character, Honoring, Attitude, Nurturing, Caring & Educate) , in which he is still the current President. He started Team Crossover Elite, which was a traveling AAU basketball program that has helped thousands of kids see the world, by playing the game of basketball. He has started several basketball leagues throughout the tri-state and Baltimore, Maryland, such as, Lil' Dribblers, DBA (Delaware Basketball Association), Stop the Violence Basketball League). In honor of two youths that participated in his leagues, James Darryl Rogers and Quiare Nesmith, that lost their lives to gun violence, he renamed the Stop the Violence Basketball Leagues, JDR and Coach Q. Coach Rob also sponsors "Me & My Dad Got Game," its a 2-on-2 Basketball Tournament for dads and their children, giving fathers and role models an opportunity to connect and build lifetime skills.

In 2014, he created a positive community magazine, New Young Mindz (NYM) in which, the youth and young adults collaborate to highlight positive things in the community. In addition to all the things Coach Rob is doing, he also writes plays that speak to young and older people regarding struggles in the urban communities of America. Coach Rob has created several outlets for youth who are not engaged in sports, through the development of a performing arts program. Providing youth of all levels of talent an opportunity to participate in the performing arts helping youth to develop "to be the best they can be no matter the odds stacked against them." This is what Coach Robs is inspired to accomplish.

In January 2018, he opened The Learning Foundation. It serves the urban community of Wilmington, and has several programs that focus on Science, Technology, Engineering, Arts and Math. The children happily frequent the establishment as a safe haven where they can feel love and have structure.

In 2019 he opened Bell Ame Beauty Lounge. It's a male and female hair salon that teaches children how to do hair. His company created 14 jobs in the city. He continues to open up businesses that are creating different avenues for people in our community to have something to look forward to.

In the words of Coach Rob, "None of what I do is done for me. I have lived through not having, not seeing people that care, no father figure with no structure in my early youth." Coach Rob's purpose is to show kids to never give up on their dreams, if you can see it, you can do it. His mission is to give every child a CHANCE. He is a father, a coach, a leader, an educator, and counselor giving himself everyday often without financial compensation or recognition. He is focusing more and more on his writing skills with more plays and movies to come. COACH ROB, he is a man of heart, honor, and humility living his life on purpose.

www.ingramcontent.com/pod-product-compliance
Lightning Source LLC
Chambersburg PA
CBHW041528120626

46551CB00018B/2620